Brewster's Big Adventure:
Seven Wonders of the World

All rights reserved.
Ryan Douglas Publishing L.L.C
Text copyright © 2021 Brewster's Big Adventure
Library of Congress Control Number: 2020925717
ISBN: 978-1-7362224-0-9

Brewster's Big Adventure: Seven Wonders of the World

There must be so many wonderful places in the world!

Inside, the TV was left on while his dad napped on the couch.

Brewster watched a show about the Seven Wonders of the World — the greatest structures ever built!

Brewster howled with delight.
He wanted to see all
Seven Wonders of the World!

United States of America

The closest World Wonder to his hometown of San Francisco, California, was down in Mexico.

So how did Brewster get there?

He took a car!

His parents drove the car while Brewster hung his head out the window.

His long tongue flapped in the wind.

After a long drive they arrived at the first World Wonder, Chichen Itza.

Chichen Itza was once a powerful city. Though the city is now a ruin (no longer in use), there was lots to explore.

The most famous building looked like a tall pyramid, with stairs up each side. They were like stairs in Brewster's own home, but much bigger!

Mexico

The next World Wonder was all the way down in Brazil.

So how did Brewster get there?

He took a boat!

He and his parents hopped onto a great big boat.

Brewster spent the whole boat ride eating his favorite gourmet meals.

After a long ride they arrived at the second World Wonder, Christ the Redeemer.

Christ the Redeemer is a gigantic statue of Jesus Christ.

The statue's arms are stretched out wide, as if in need of a hug!

Brewster tried to give him a hug, but no matter how hard he tried he couldn't wrap his paws around the huge statue!

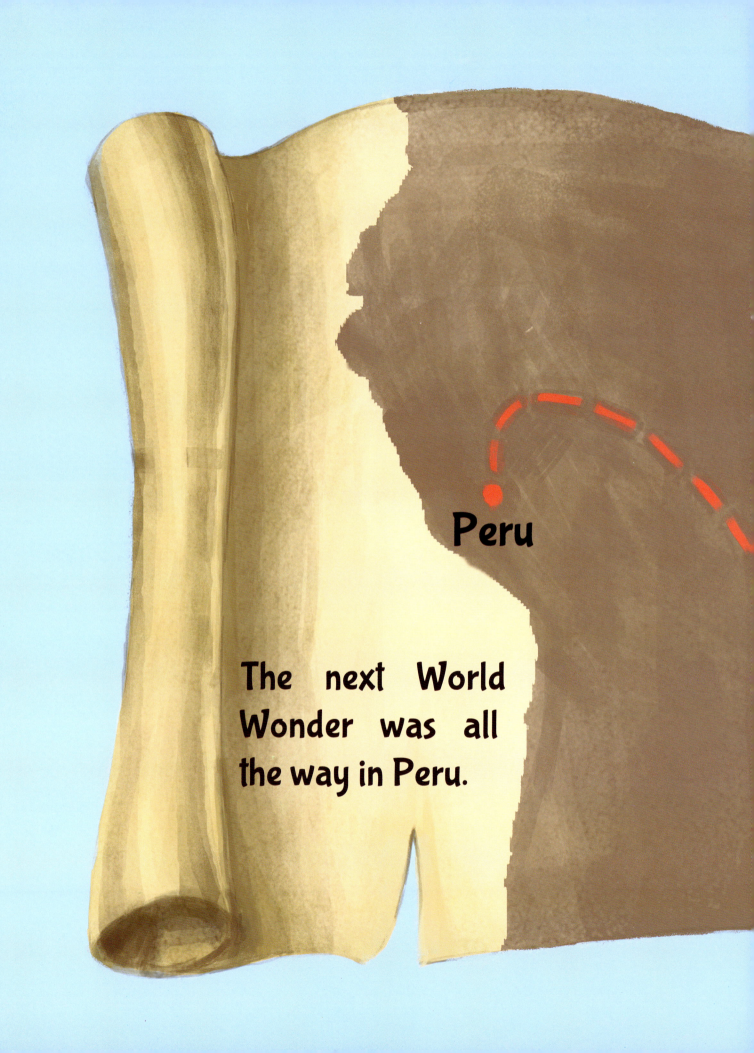

Peru

The next World Wonder was all the way in Peru.

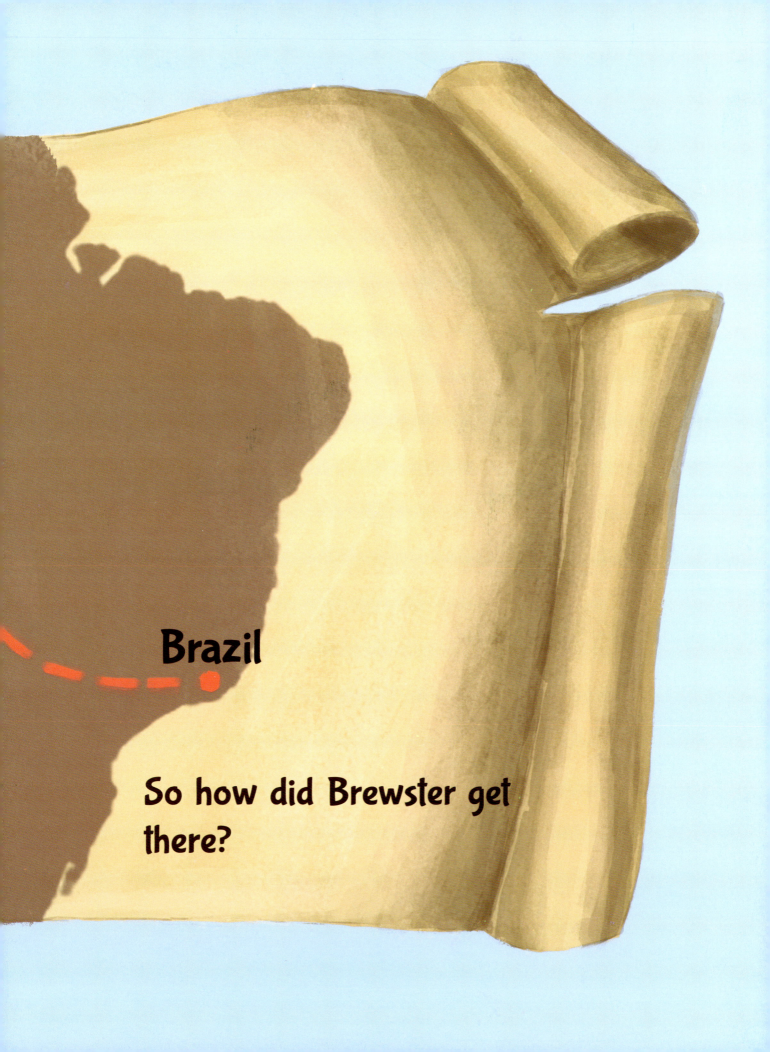

He took a bus!

The bus was full of friendly tourists who taught Brewster and his parents the local language, Spanish.

After a long bus ride he arrived at the third World Wonder, Machu Picchu. When Brewster arrived, he said gracias — thank you — to the bus driver!

Machu Picchu was once a city. The city was lost for many years, which seemed silly to Brewster.

Brewster had lost small toys before but he never would've lost something as big as a city!

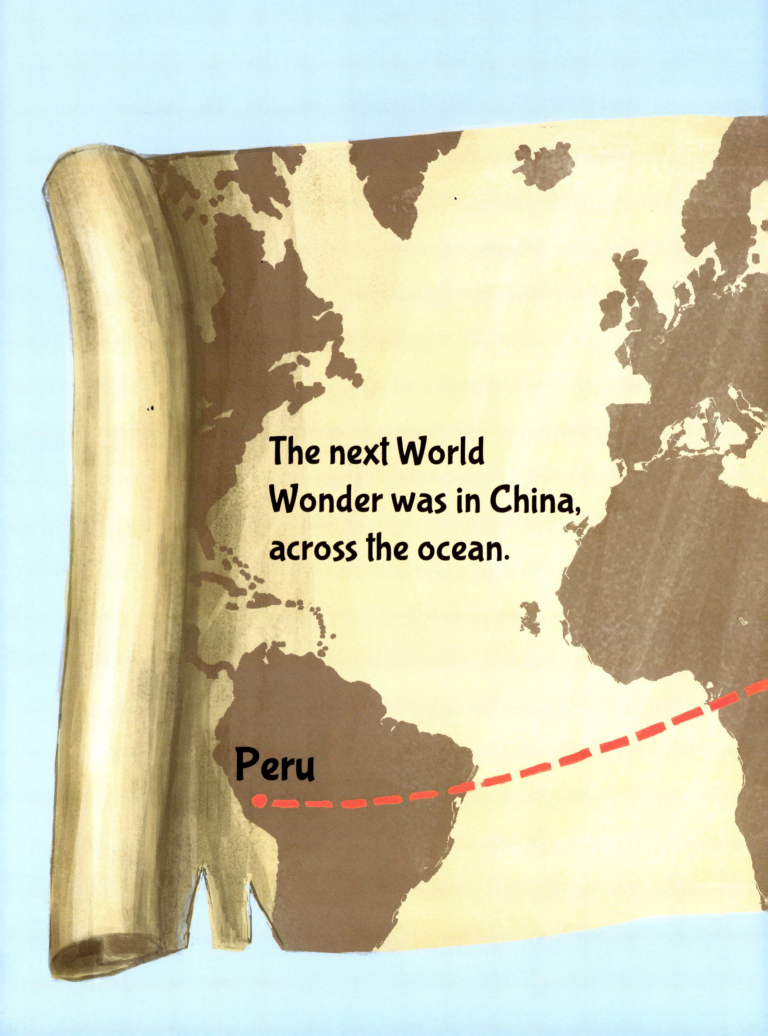

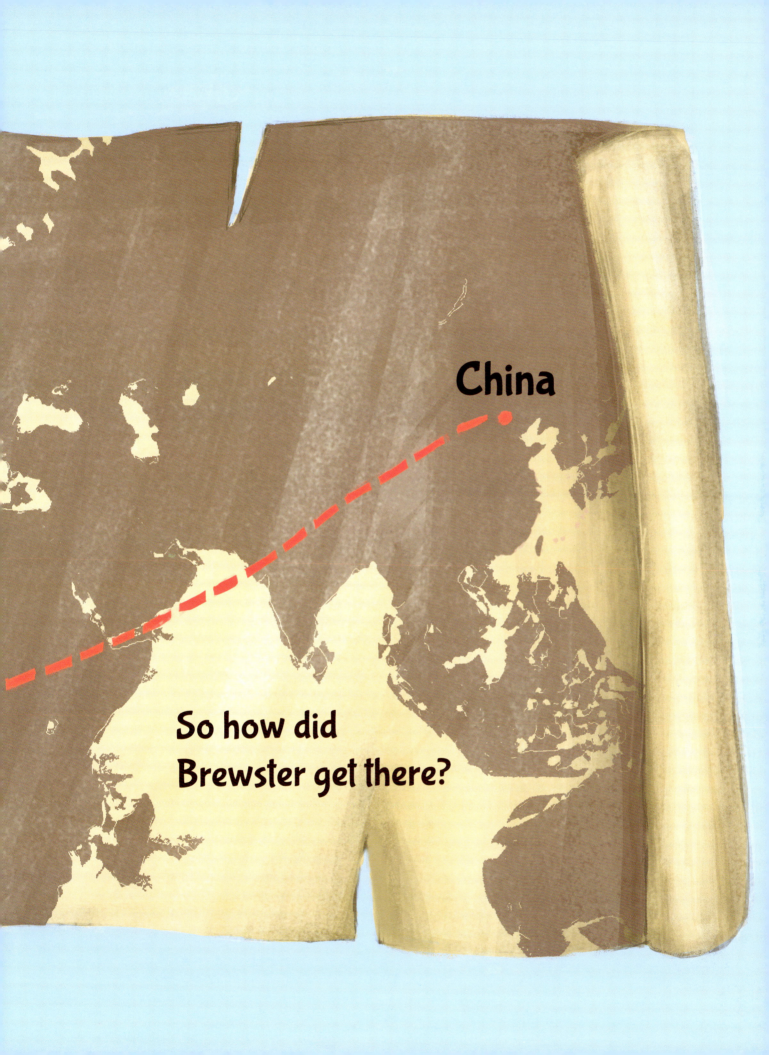

He took a plane!

He looked out the window at all the beautiful clouds. One cloud even looked like his home!

He missed his home but that was okay. Brewster would be there soon.

After a long plane ride he arrived at the fourth World Wonder, The Great Wall of China.

The Great Wall was built to protect the whole northern border of one of the world's largest countries, China.

The wall was over 13,000 miles long. That would be like walking from one coast of the United States to the other — five times!

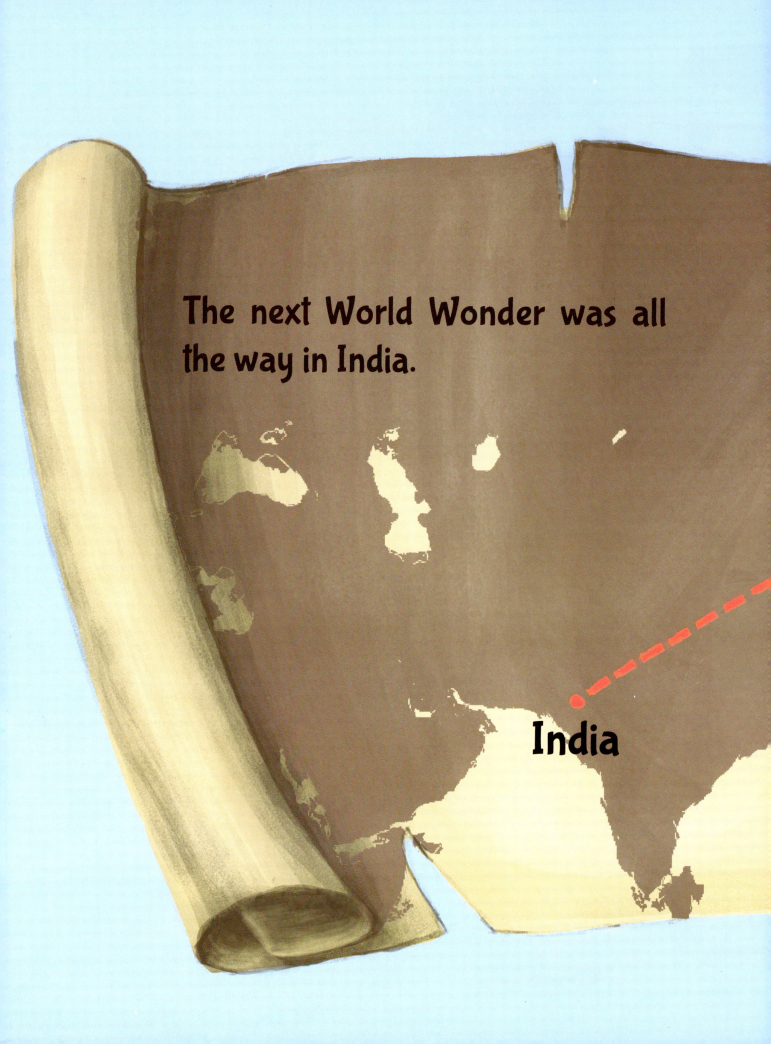
The next World Wonder was all the way in India.

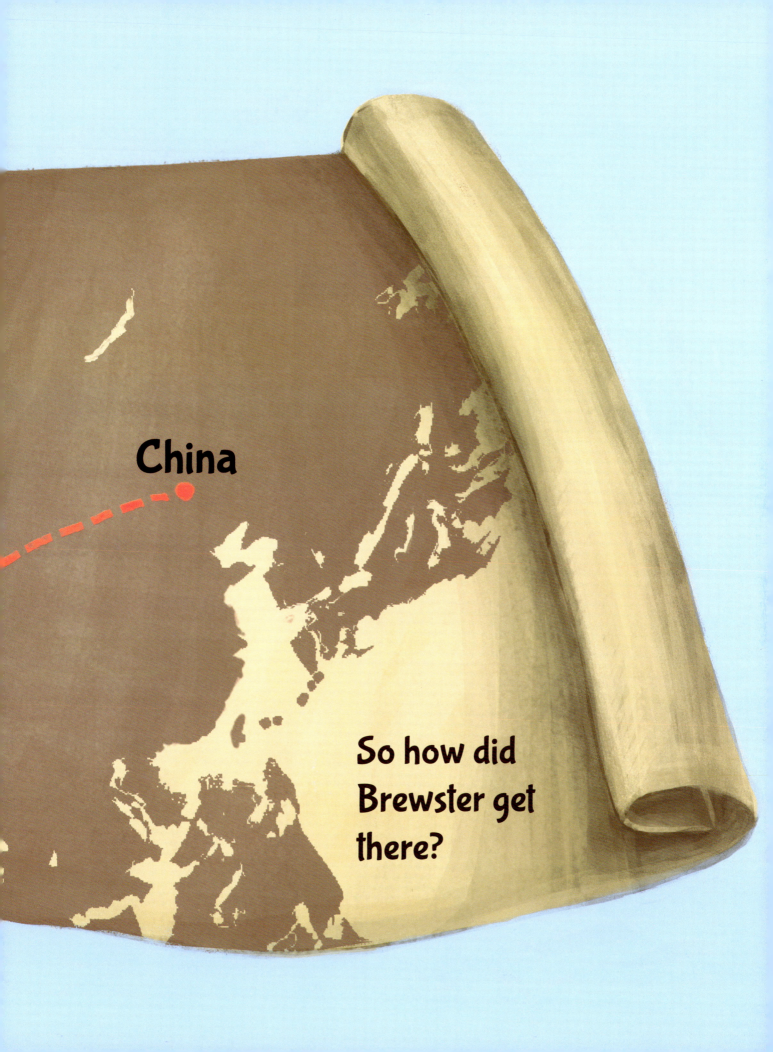

He took a helicopter!

The helicopter flew up, down, forwards, backwards, and side to side.

After a long helicopter ride, Brewster and his parents arrived at the fifth World Wonder, the Taj Mahal.

India was very hot, but the Taj Mahal was white as snow.

From far away it looked like the beautiful dome top was a giant snowball!

Brewster wished he had a snow ball to cool off with!

Instead he gazed in the reflecting pool, and thought he would like to go for a swim when he arrived back home.

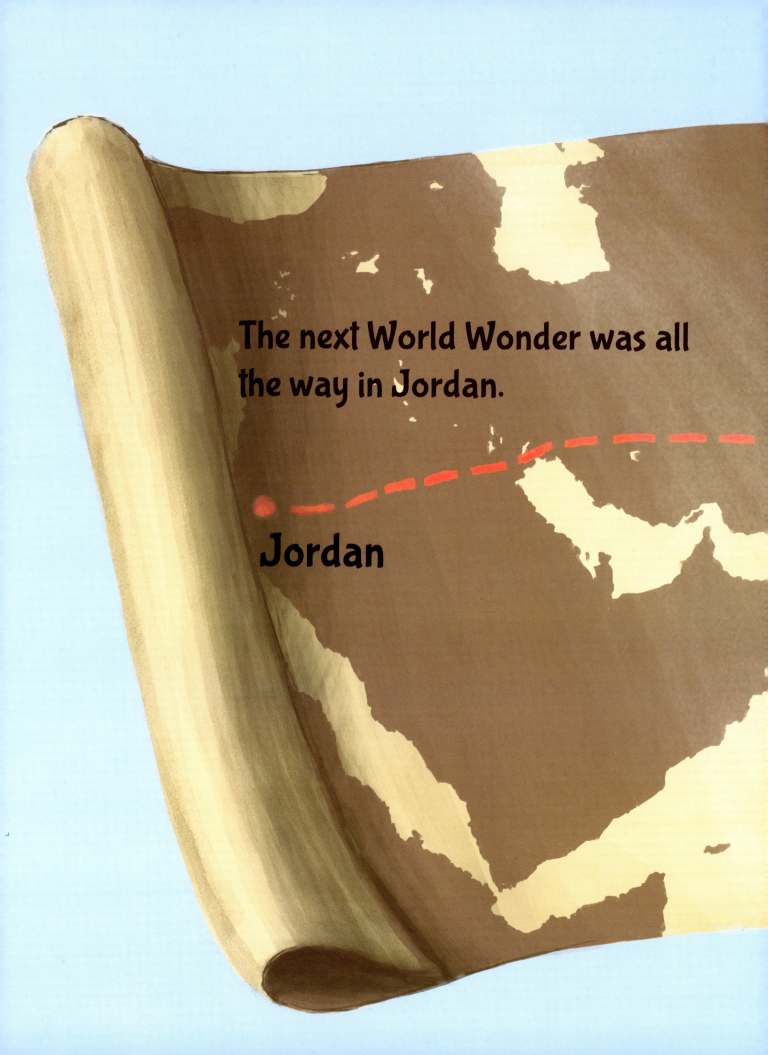

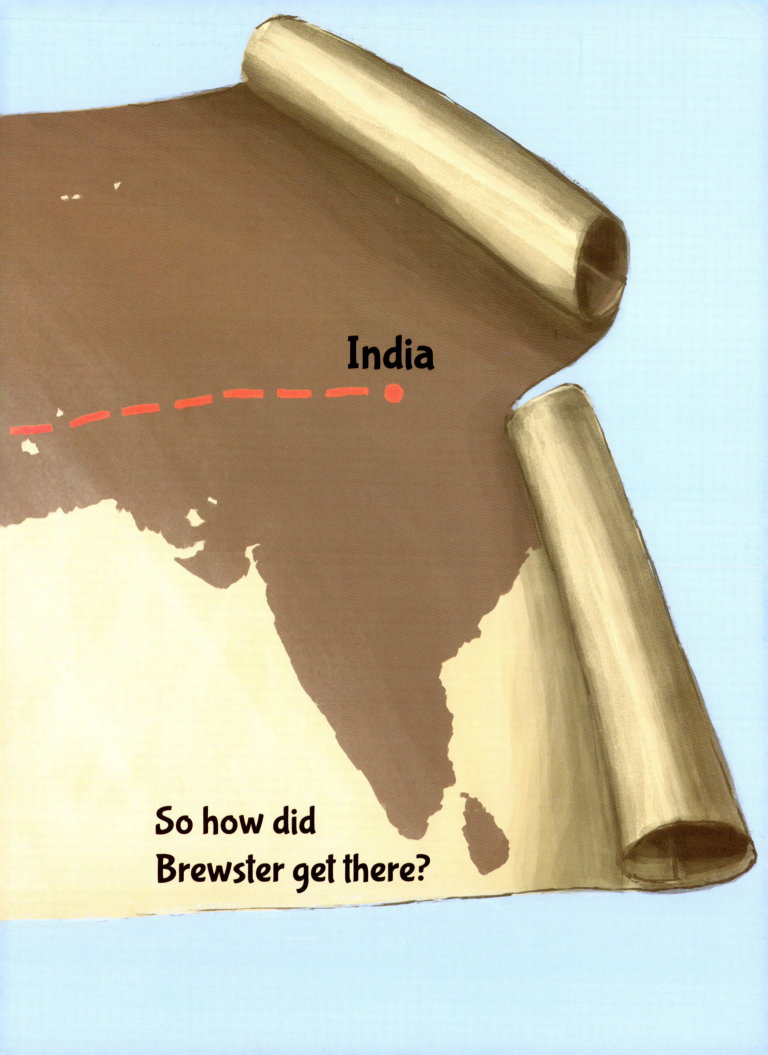

He took a motorcycle!

Brewster's parents hopped on a shiny, red motorcycle while Brewster rode in the side car. Together they rode over tall mountains and through hot deserts.

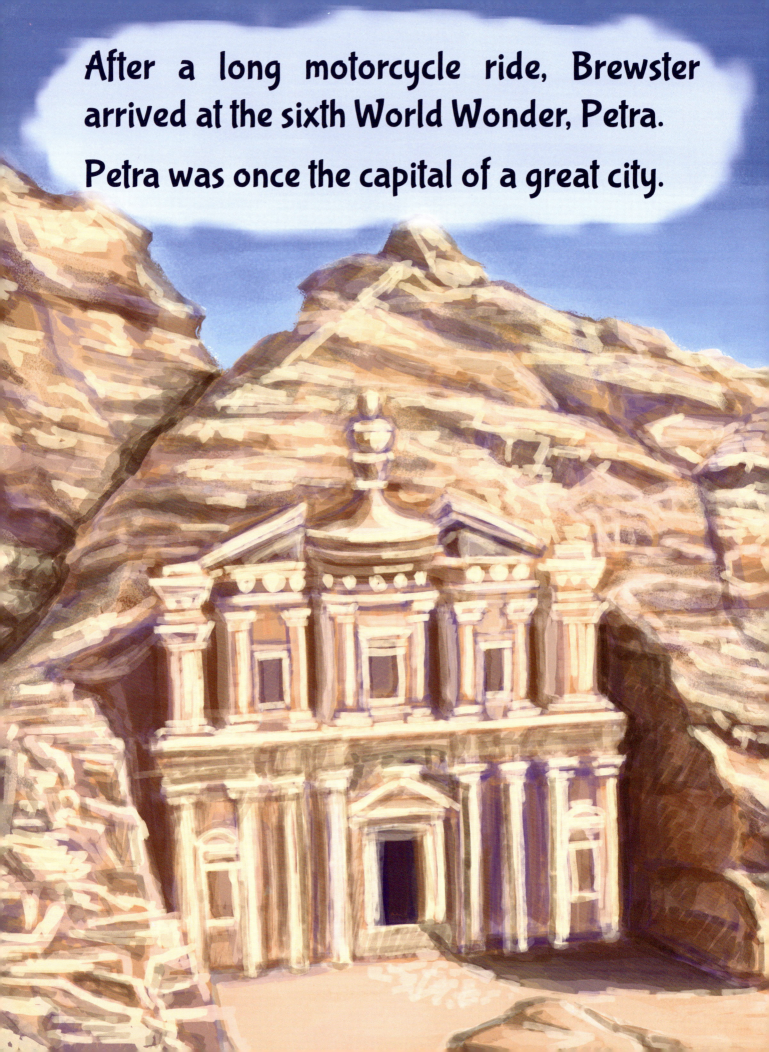

After a long motorcycle ride, Brewster arrived at the sixth World Wonder, Petra. Petra was once the capital of a great city.

Some experts say Petra is 2,500 years–old. In comparison, Brewster is only 3 years–old.

Petra was carved into the mountain like a sculpture, making it one of the world's most impressive structures.

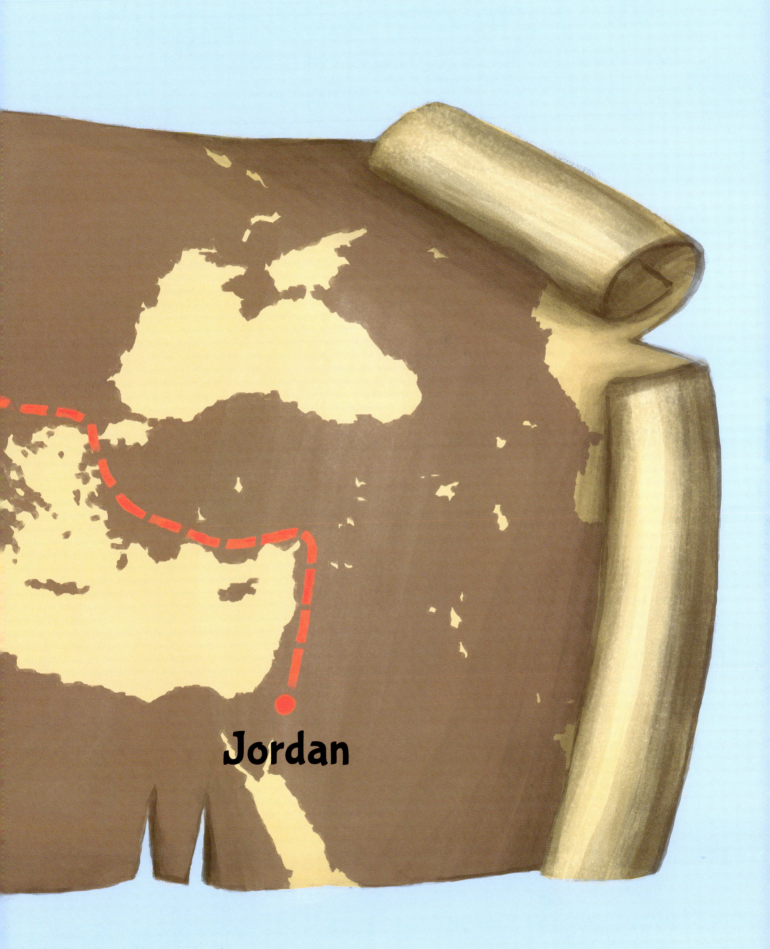

He took a train! Brewster got to see lots of new countries and make new friends.

After a long train ride, Brewster and his parents arrived at the seventh and final World Wonder, the Colosseum.

The Colosseum was a stadium once used for sporting events.

It reminded him of the baseball stadiums at home but this one was way older.

It was used for five hundred years!

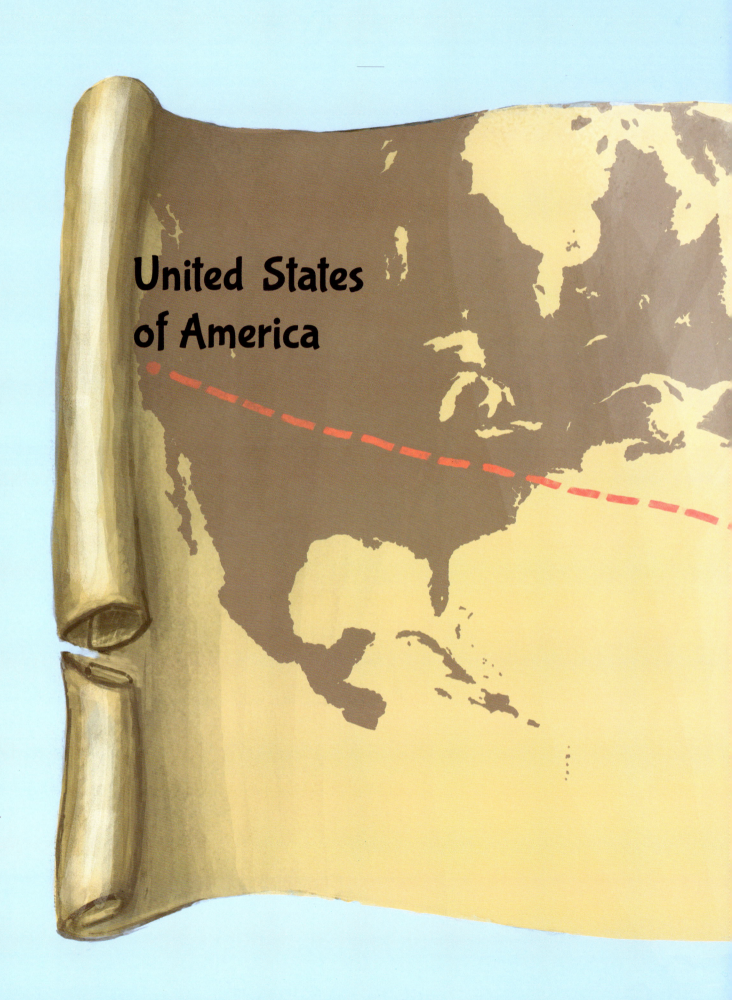

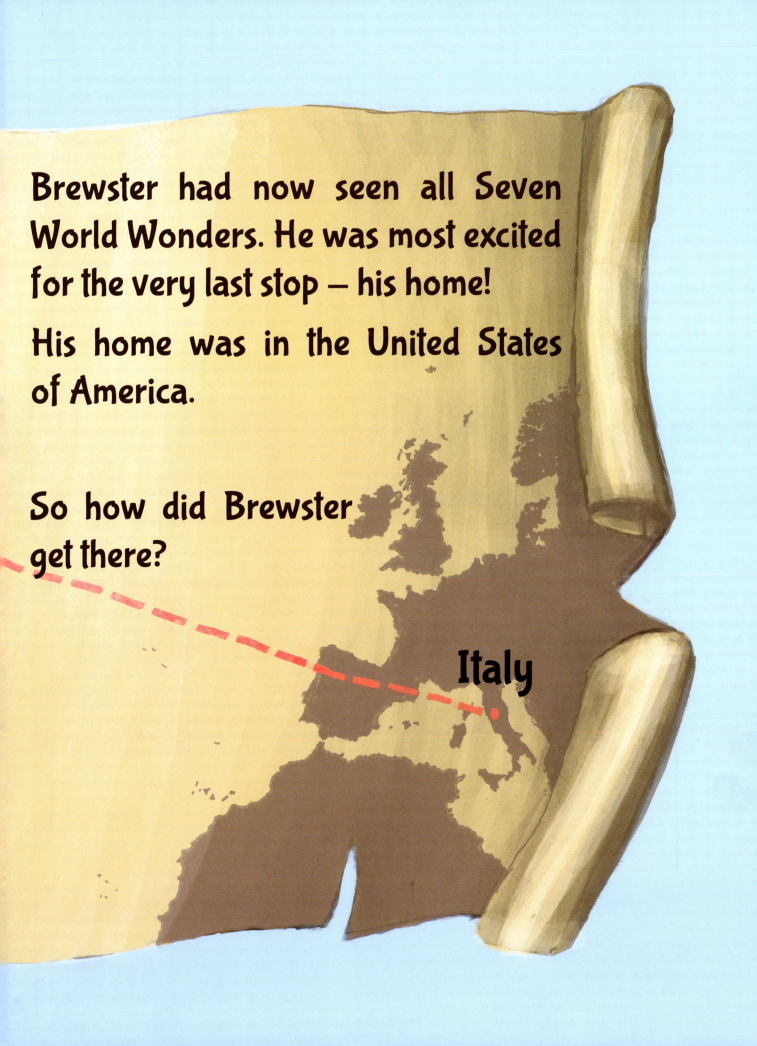

Brewster had now seen all Seven World Wonders. He was most excited for the very last stop — his home!

His home was in the United States of America.

So how did Brewster get there?

Italy